I PITCHED A TENT IN HELL

Taylor Barton

Taylor Barton

© Copyright 2021

ISBN: 9798667673552

Dedicated to:

Josephine Lee Smith

The Songs

ECHO
NOT THE KIND YOU KEEP
LOST LUCY
BEEN IN A STORM
*DON'T QUIT
MIDFLIGHT
VAPOR
GOD BROKE UP WITH ME
HALEY
HE FLIES BY
MEN
DARKNESS MAKES ME STRONG
WILD OLD FOOL
THOROUGHBRED
MS. THIRD PLACE
HEARTACHE ON THE HUDSON
THE CALLING
WIND
HIM
7 STEPS
WHERE DID YOU GO
I'M THE ANGEL YOU TURNED AWAY
FOR THOSE AMONG US
THE WHEATFIELDS
LAST TIME

FOREWORD

I love songs. Songs reveal different aspects of my mind. Nothing is in the present, nothing in the past, nothing linear. Songs are altruistic, forgiving and fortuitous. For me they reveal a deeper, darker, richer interior, rarely present in conversation. Songs embody fantasy and reality. They are conceived out of yearning; sometimes, they are my confessions of sins and sometimes secret desires.

Contents

1.

ECHO

I hold daily communion with my three animals while I meditate each morning. They look forward to the ritual with great enthusiasm. My big, fat, tabby parks himself on my chest and places his paws around my neck. He loves to be as close to me as he can and I love to feel his heartbeat with mine. The Maine coon cats, (the devils' links) assemble themselves likewise on my stomach and legs. Their purring eases my breath and I fall into a deeper trance.

All practitioners suggest one mediates with the back upright or sitting in a lotus position but my God, (God of Art), doesn't require such rigidity. My God asks that I keep an open heart. The muses hover above my head and give me my daily instruction. They pose the turbulent questions?

"What can I create today? How can I rise above my mediocrity? Can I rid myself of the ever-draining depression that drags me down; down, like a fisherman overboard with waders."

Inevitably, I have to focus on the positive thoughts drifting in and out because my earthly desire is to forget trying and just go back to sleep. My cats think a day in bed sounds like the perfect plan. As I receive my feline's unconditional love, the best love I might ever get, I formulate a plan with my inner committee. I want to worship melody. I want to be the vehicle of lyric. I want the world to hear the melody and lyric I am hearing. The muses and I are co-creators and we have something to say.

I feel myself drifting towards their dreams. I want to bring them to fruition. I want to be a woman strong enough and centered enough to run her own country. A goddess who is self-sufficient and capable of toppling an empire; my dreams are rebuffed by my reality. My husband is the God in our house. He is the value and he makes the money. Ultimately, it is my husband everyone sees.

ECHO

Am I still here, a shadow of your fear?
Am I that small, your silhouettes' wall?

I'm not an echo, not a picture on a pond
I can take you down, down where you belong
I'm not an echo, but the current of a lake
I will take you down, down to your true mate

A lunar eclipse, shades your big, bold ship
A wintering, rain? Your mirror locked in chains

Chorus

Thru the echo of your call, I became the queen's law
Better dig a little bit deeper, I'm your heart's keeper.

Chorus

I will take you down, down, down.

It was a gorgeous, sunny evening, humid but clear. We were in Positano, Italy, parked adjacent to a soccer field. I sat on the bus with a yellow legal pad getting ready to journal my daily thoughts. The boys were sound checking, sans Bob, as Bob never showed up until an hour before they played. The initial bliss of my romance had soured but I was enchanted with rock n' roll and though my relationship was suffering, I had been writing lyrics as a way to feel connected to the trip, as being the girlfriend of the sideman was losing its luster. I was very busy studying the twentieth century prophet; Dylan.

I will never meet or witness a more committed artist. He was well versed in his craft. He moved me every night. It was never the same song and he never sang them the same either. His songs were like epiphanies; they hit like lightning. I wondered if Jesus was as provocative. I wondered if I was like Mary

Magdalene who had relinquished her ideology and forfeited her life to follow Christ's prophecy?

It was hard to digest the daily excitement of touring with the most famous troubadour. It was hard to adjust to A-list ways coming from a gypsy, chorus girl existence. It was a difficult role to play. "I must be demure in spirit, seductive in garb, and never contrary to the itinerary." Whining or fighting was off limits. I became a sophisticated, savvy road-dog.

GE started playing a blues number. I settled in to write. I was lonely in Italy. I did not like the feeling of being invisible. The production manager and I had our daily chat but I felt like a wallflower.

We had just arrived after a sixteen-hour haul from San Sebastian, Spain where Basque extremists had tried to terrorize Bob. Dressed in orange turbans, they hurled large boulders and rocks at our bus. Bob had left in a different bus, camouflaged for war. The night before that, we were in Madrid, staying at The Four Seasons across the street from the Prado. I got my first glimpse of Goya while I was jogging around the topiary gardens which were meticulously manicured by the Museum.

I felt like I was slowly disintegrating. There was nothing on the road that kept me anchored in my own reality. I was no longer confident or secure in public. I was afraid of being alone. I was afraid of being separated from GE. I had to go to Greece alone after Rome while the band was going on to Turkey. My friends at home thought I was the luckiest girl alive but I felt inadequate.

NOT THE KIND YOU KEEP

I'm getting tired of quick remarks, sorry darling I'm in the dark
Look I guess its time to face the truth, time to leave no time to
lose,
I can carry my load down one more lane
I'm weary and spent, from playing the game
I'm not the kind you keep lying up on a shelf
Not a gleaming gold trophy, collecting the dust

Chorus

Won't you please darling let me be free
If I would choose your life, it would strangle me
With your cares all gone, well there's nothing to do
Break these chains of love and move on thru.

You're not my kind babe, you're pretending for me
It was a dangerous spark that ignited this dream
So, let this scene drift off let the pain set in
It's too much weight for this girl to sustain
Bye baby, I'll miss you tonight, bye, bye baby it's not worth the
fight
I'll miss you're sweet, sweet, loving, your touch, your tunes
Bye baby, keep playing your blues
Chorus

As for me well things are always the same
I keep moving in circles, but changing the names
Like the tides retreat, it's rather sublime
It's rough underneath I'm not the keeping kind
I'm disappointed at my dealing with fate
The time I realized love, it's always too late
I left the gates too soon I missed the crucial signs
Guess I'm learning to live, I'm passing the time

Boston has always been a big part of my history. When I was thirteen I ran away from Baltimore to Brookline, Massachusetts. I stayed with a girl I had met at tennis camp named Meredith, and took refuge there when I was very unhappy in my adolescence because of confusing feelings. Buried feelings that I was unconsciously avoiding because my then boyfriend, Pip, had dumped me after one kiss. I was unsure if it was the shame spilling off of my lips or worse, another untouched virgin he desired.

I might have lost a boyfriend but Pip introduced me to Jerry Garcia when I was twelve and I became an official Dead head, owning every disc thereafter. I would meet Jerry Garcia fifteen years later, backstage at Neil Young's annual concert to benefit his son's disease. Garcia played "friend of the devil" real slow for me. Rob Wasserman's wife would become my manager for a short time. It would be Pip who later entered the music business and distributed my CD, *Skinny Kat.* Coincidentally, he had the same last name as GE.

Meredith appeared back in my life thirty years later, just in time to photograph four out of five CD covers. So, I ran away spending my days in the Boston Commons, sleeping at night in Meredith's boyfriend's car. My sister, Mandy, was attending Andover. I was trying to get closer to her because I missed her after she was abruptly yanked from school and sent away. Her empty bedroom haunted me. Mandy never returned to Maryland so subsequently, I always visited her in Boston. I had become a dancer, my only source of bodily self-esteem, and would often take classes at 'The Joy of Movement Center' when I was near Cambridge.

One June, I was there and the dancers were talking about an older, (twenty) blonde dancer. They said she was Cat Stevens old girlfriend, that she was a misfit, debutante from Ann Arbor who dated Cat Stevens before he became a Muslim. "Wild World" was apparently written about her. I was a debutante too and I had played "Tea for the Tillerman" to death. I was mesmerized by the girl's story. The dancers also said she was no longer rich but poverty stricken, strung out, and stripping in the red-light district. Her name was Lucy. I thought she was pretty, actually beautiful. I meditated on that, while dancing for years after. I wrote "Lost Lucy" when I turned thirty-two.

My first gig with Generic Blondes outside of New York was at the House of Blues in Cambridge, Massachusetts. I was relaying the backlog to the song when some guy yelled out, "I knew that girl Lucy. She stripped in my Dad's club. I heard she was a cop in Pennsylvania now." Sometimes I think the song is more about me than her.

LOST LUCY

Girl from Ann Arbor
Landed in the harbor
Settled down in Boston
Over-exhaustion
Dated a rocker
Who was strong enough to stop her
He took her belongings
Left her full of longing

Chorus

Lost Lucy, take this as a warning
You can't warn a wild born again
Though I saw God, shining in her hair
She never knew he was resting there

Saw her dancing in the combat zone
Drunk and dazed in a world of her own
A runaway, so reckless and loose
Giving it out on in peep-show booth

Chorus

It was cold and gray when they retrieved her that morning

You can't warn a wild born again

Guess she's free, now that she's dead

I think she smiled when she turned God's head

Lost Lucy, so fragile and fair

Found it hard, with God in her hair

Everyone felt robbed of her face

Of Lucy's gaze and Lucy's grace

Chorus

2.
MIDFLIGHT

I was four or five when Martin Luther King got assassinated. Baltimore was on a curfew and looting was a daily practice during the following, volatile summer. My father worked downtown and was friendly with the Black community. He somehow had acquired a black and white, Reverend King film that was being circulated to progressive thinkers. My father was not a normal, white suburban man. He mixed well with the racially challenged Metropolitan. My father had a huge influence on my political outlook and his was one of tolerance and peace. He was a maverick for his time because although he was a Republican, he was the only man I knew in Maryland who didn't start and finish his week with a gin and tonic; sober his entire life.

When I was twelve I was sent to tennis camp just outside Squaw Valley, the northern side of Nevada; Incline Village to be specific. It was there I met Dexter and Marty King, the two sons of the great civil rights' leader. Having their father etched in my brain as a hero, naturally I was drawn to the two famous heirs. I don't feel that the counselors or campers shared my opinion. Racism still ran deep, in the seventies, even though great strides had been accomplished due to their father's demise.

I had a school girl affair with Dexter and we started a thing. Kissing was the extent of it, before an older counselor swept me off my feet. I think the King boys left and I stayed on for another session as I was being groomed to be the next Chrissy Everett.

We were assigned a speech in my junior year of high school. I did the "*I have a dream*" speech. I find it easy to understand King's position. Although, white, upper-class, well educated, and a budding debutante, I viscerally understood the mentality of the oppressed. I had bonded with our maid and I heard the multitude of transgressions she had survived. And I loved our maid more than I loved my mother. Lucy, had been the maid of my grand-mother, my mother, and then went on to be my oldest sister's. She gave me real love, gave me encouragement, and supported my every endeavor. I loved the cherry-freckled, charcoal of her skin and her southern drawl. She gave me hope, desire, and her utter attention; nothing that any one relative ever attempted.

Poetry was my way of speaking to myself. I had a journal in which I scrawled lyrics of wanting to live or die or both. I was either highly artistic or suicidal. Here was the song that came from that experience. It was based, in part, from my Martin Luther King fascination and a William Turner painting that I was intoxicated with.

BEEN IN A STORM

In my dream, I see a beam
In my dream, it's calling peace
In my dream, I feel the key
In my dream, we can be free

Chorus
This place, this place inside of me
Is space, a space that's lost at sea.

In my dream, I see a queen
In my dream, she whispers things
In my dream, a small child sings
In my dream, she's wearing wings
This place, this place inside of me,
Is space, a space that's lost at sea.

I've been in a storm so long
I've been in a storm so long, children
I've been in a storm so long
Oh, give me little time to pray
Yes, give me little time to pray.

My father was not unlike Robert Duvall in that old southern movie, "The Great Santini". He was a military man who avoided the war with a falsely diagnosed case of tuberculosis. He had gone through the training and was scheduled to be deported but was quickly and abruptly assigned to quarantine, after Boot camp in South Carolina. He was "a cocked gun, left on friendly territory".

I come from a long line of southerners, Robert E. Lee on my mother's side and John Marshall on my father's. My father's great, grandfather had several boys, four that passed in the same battle in Virginia during the Civil War; stoicism, soldiering, and sarcasm are a part of my cellular make up. Southerners rely on the 3H's; homilies, humor, and habit to get through life. Many of my memories are wrapped around homilies that my father barked at us. He was constantly advising me, "even a blind pig could find an acorn sometimes." He loved to give me anecdotes that would conjure up winning. He was dead set on my athletic skills as my means to achieve something in life. "Don't be a birdbrain!" was his affectionate phrase. I was very dutiful to him because if I crossed him, I would be left with my borderline mother who had posed as a clinical psychologist to avoid the nuthouse.

One day, my father was feeling especially fond of me because I had acquired a tennis trophy. During our goodnights, he would deliver scrappy pieces of paper that illustrated prose from a super-achiever. With half -of -a Christian prayer, he would send me to dreamland with the expectation of an Olympian. I remember one vividly. It was just a poem, cut out of Reader's Digest and since it was given with sincerity, I took it to mean, something of great value. I pasted it on black construction paper and nailed it into my flowery wallpaper.

It was my favorite homily and I still get choked up when I sing it because it reminds me of my father. It remains the defining wisdom that he tried to impart.

DON' T QUIT

Author Unknown

When things go wrong as they sometimes will
When the road you're treading seems all uphill
Funds are low, and the debts are high
And you want to smile but you have to sigh
When things are getting you down a bit
Rest if you must, but don't you quit

Life seems queer with its twists and turns
And many of us often learn
We could have captured the victory cup
Had we fought for a while and not given up
When care is pressing you down a bit
Rest if you must, don't you quit.

Success is failure turned inside out

The silver tint on the clouds of doubt

And you never can tell how close you are

It may be near when it seems so far

Stick to the fight when you are hardest hit

When things are getting wrong, you must not quit

Rest if you must, no don't you quit.

I loved religion. On a daily basis, I tried very hard to elevate myself out of suburbia through religion. I believed love existed, as I found lovers' carved notes on the wood of many hemlocks, but love eluded me. I put my faith in the unknown.

When I was seven, I dragged a log out in the backyard, set it up as my pulpit, and practiced preaching to my initial audience; my sisters and sheepdog. I think every performer emulates a prophet, and I was no different. I tried to find myself through every prophet available; Christ, Buddha, writers, painters, poets, you name it.

My sisters would scream, "Shut up and stop singing." My sisters weren't very impressed and thought I was wasting my time. They found their God in food, drugs, money or work. Oddly, I was the only one interested in ascending. My mother was a pseudo Christian and my father, an atheist. It would have been easier to side with my father but if I had nothing larger than my world to believe in, I would have killed myself right then.

It was never an actual living prophet I emulated. I wanted to touch immortality. I wanted to be immortal. I basically couldn't stand living in my own skin. I don't know why, but I felt deprived like the downtrodden, and was sure that sooner or later, enlightenment would release me from pent up frustration with the emptiness I experienced growing up. I had my eye on one thing; height. I loved to climb mountains to escape the chaos. I loved to get high. I wanted to be with a God who could release me. I often dreamed that I could fly.

MIDFLIGHT

Under a tree, I wait and see
I know you're no longer in the cathedrals
I know that Jesus abandoned all those steeples

Are you lost off you cross?
You've fallen one step behind
Are you the holy shield in my mind?
to know a trace of your grace

Why do people need to be stoned?
Why are we so fractured and so alone?

Will you show, on a road?

I've waited all these years

I was hoping you might appear

To know your name outside a frame,

To know your name, to know your name

Carved in a tree.

3.

HALEY

New Orleans has always held its allure based on magic and music. It is a country unto itself, and pre-Katrina, the most flamboyant cesspool I ever visited. I had signed with a small label there in 1997 and made a handful of trips to showcase myself in the Quarter's roadhouses. The stench of beer permeated the streets and there was an incessant sound of trumpets. Horn players blaring "When the Saints, Come Marching In", were accompanied by tap dancers painted in white powder. Beignets and chicory coffee spilled out of French cafes and a warm breeze blew a putrid scent in from the Mississippi.

The graveyards, with their statues and tombs above ground, were constant reminders of the drunken ghosts that were eternally masquerading at Mardi Gras.

GE and I were opening for Louis Armstrong's grandson and Sonny Landreth. We were in the House of Blues Annex called "The Church." Much of my time was spent in observation, drinking

in the Creole living and as much as I loved it, I distrusted it.
Voodoo dolls and black magic scared me. I was not into the devil
nor wanted to invite sin into my life. In fact, I already had enough
bad luck on my own, and didn't need to taunt the devil or hoodoos
for more. A lot of my love was based on fantasies. I loved places I
couldn't get to, like the moon. People I could never meet like the
Dalai Lama, things I would never have, like money and power.
Even my muses had hoodwinked me into believing I was going to
be BIG. I should've known I was destined for barely marginal
because everyone who lived in New Orleans, knew it was the
greatest place to make a career out of 'not having' a career.

On the bus, (we actually had a tour bus once,) I wrote this
song. We had finished the Jazz Fest and were headed to Atlanta.

VAPOR

You crept in, an amorous vapor
A cool breeze, a slinky savoir
You drift by, a spooky hipster
A French King, a hoodoo minister

Vapor

Desire circles like a prayer
I want to touch, you're not there

Are you a ghost I can feel?

Am I the host you came to steal?

Vapor

Chorus

I dream through the night

We ride in twilight

With stars in our eyes

Dawn will be my demise

Bells are ringing double-time

My heart is pumping twisted rhymes

You crucify my mind

Chorus

You swept out like a tempest

Headed for the hills of Memphis

You departed like a hearse

Blacked dust or a wicked curse

Vapor

Were you my savoir?

I have struggled with depression my whole life. I am the most high-functioning depressive that I know. I envy those who can't get out of bed. Despite my self-loathing, I have my daughter. I have to get up for her.

I watch the commercials for all the anti-depressants competing for a chance to induce euphoria but even the drug companies know that anti-depressants are just band-aids; chemistry is stronger. And while the doctors hand these mind-altering drugs out like candy, it behooves me that no pharmaceutical companies have thought of the obvious, by running blood tests on their likely candidates to see what combination of serotonin, or whatever, is the right match.

I have tried the various brands. Paxil made me feel like a zombie and I couldn't sleep; Prozac was like speed; Seroquel was a ticket to a psychotic breakdown. Xanax was for amateurs. And then there was Lexapro. Middle of the road, everything was tolerable, coasting for years, until I noticed I'd lost my artistry, my vocabulary, my sense of humor, my desire to pursue anything; and myself.

While I was tackling my homicidal rage that always accompanied my PMS, I decided when my daughter was very young, that she didn't deserve the tirades that my depression loved to showcase. So, I signed up for an anger workshop at a well-known facility that caters to all kinds of addictions and dysfunction. Depression is really suppressed anger with a biological flare for internal fireworks.

I arrived on a Friday evening to find I had a corner room on the top floor of a stone-cobbled mansion. I had been to this place before for a workshop for families of addiction, so I was familiar with the setting and brought my arsenal for what one might consider utter deprivation. Many other buildings housed for the addictive clients wouldn't allow cell phones, sweet 'n' low or sugar, so I had it all stashed.

I had a petite roommate, who was very sweet and gentle. I kept reminding myself we were not at Canon Ranch but a weekend with people who acknowledged they needed help without being remanded by courts to jail.

My roommate told me one of the saddest tales of an upbringing that I had ever heard, (and I have heard everything). Her life was so heartbreaking.

She said that when she was four her mother and she were in a car-crash and her mother had died. She had sustained such physical injuries that had caused her massive pain for the rest of her life. Her father had remarried and her stepmother physically abused her. She was married now and her only daughter was a drug addict. Her husband believed in "tough love" and threw their child out of the house, as he was sober and had the know-how of addicts. She was crushed with the weight of her history, the loss of her daughter, and yes, depressed.

I don't think whatever story I might tell would elicit feelings of compassion, as I saw my life, as one of privilege. I just had bad genes. On the contrary, shrinks had told me, they were surprised I lived this long.

We were going about our workshops and my roommate was in another group so I didn't see her in the day, however, the second evening, as a means to revive us from the gut-wrenching excavations being conducted on our souls, they started to play some form of psychic musical chairs. I refused to participate. I sat it out, unobserved.

My roommate seemed very happy and exuberant. I felt she must have made major progress during that day. I, on the other hand, had participated in the re-enactment of my pseudo funeral because at the core of my rage, lay suicidal desires. To ward off my propensity for this self-infliction, the group acted as my family attending my wake.

That Sunday I cut out early as I always do, because I am terrible with endings. I hate good-byes, closure, and anything that makes me feel circular. I have always needed to feel that I can leave anything at any time.

My roommate, on the other hand, needed a ride back to NYC. She was beaming from her newly won independence of rage and bantering about people walking on our roof the evening before. I heard absolutely nothing and assumed she was nuts.

Out I went, looking at the roof overshadowing our room. I went back into the house and asked the counselors if people had been walking on the roof last night. They confirmed, yes, some inmates, from another building had broken out of their corridors, to "smoke with the stars". I took it to mean some celebrity was in house, stomping overhead, while I snoozed in a deep coma from dancing with my demons.

I drove back to my life and decided suicide was not an option. I would just be condemned to myself. I wondered about my roommate from time to time but never contacted her, even though, I knew she lived nearby.

Six months after, I picked up *The Post* and on page 3, I noticed an ad with a picture, saying this girl, (my former roommate) was missing. It was a day after Easter and she had been gone since Good Friday. I was mortified.

I felt compelled to go to the police, as there were a few more details she had told me about her husband that now, seemed pertinent.

A detective asked, "Well, how do you know her"?

I didn't think the "weekend at the ANGER retreat" sounded convincing but I said, "please look at her husband! She would never have left her daughter." He scribbled the information and dismissed me as a non-event.

Three weeks later her body turned up in the East River. The Medical Examiner ruled it, a suicide. Apparently, she just jumped in the East River at FDR and 96th, they suspected, on Maundy Thursday and started swimming, until she sank. She washed up near Riker's Island.

I couldn't believe it. I wanted to call her daughter and tell her how much her mother loved her. She seemed cured that autumn weekend. I was the one that was suicidal. Strangely, I was the one that was saved. I imagined her thoughts after she succeeded in ending her life.

GOD BROKE UP WITH ME

On the shores of death were roses reign

In the fields of burnt sugarcane

On the dunes with the scattered skulls

In the wind where the bells toll

Chorus

I cry, I cannot breathe

I crash down

God broke up with me

In the dark I am flying west

Neon fish dart, the tides crest

On the lip of the coldest wave

I French-kiss a human slave

Chorus

From the hills of the deepest canyon

I view heaven as a northern lake

Buried under the leaves of abandon

Daguerreotypes of my thousand mistakes

On the shores where the roses reign

I lie in the darkest shame

I made fatal errors during my young adulthood; unwanted pregnancies. I told myself, I couldn't be a mother because of my young age. I needed to postpone motherhood for some big dream of being a chorus girl. In hindsight, it was thoroughly ridiculous. All through my twenties and thirties, I was sentenced to an invisible prison, all because I was obsessed with being noticed by strangers; strangers who lurked in theaters because we (the audience and I) both had a need to live by fantasy.

For what!? I didn't want fame. I didn't want to be in the limelight. I just wanted to be heard. I look back over the last thirty years and see nothing of great value. I have stacks of plays that were never published and sparsely performed. I wrote a novel that cost me my relationship with my father. I have ten awards from ASCAP. I made ten Cd's that wiped a savings of over hundred thousand dollars. I gave up motherhood for nothing. End result; I took the wrong path and it haunted me non-stop.

I had a friend who had racked up massive credit for writing her critically acclaimed novels, who adopted a little Chinese girl. I was in a writing workshop with her. We weren't very close but she spearheaded me into adoption. On one level it made total sense to atone for all my past sins. On another, it seemed absurd to adopt as my husband had given up a child when he was seventeen and neither one of us had an ounce of maturity between us.

God is bigger and better than my efforts and my mistakes. I was called to the plate to decide to reverse all my misdoings. I was given a second chance to try love and walk virgin terrain, and find that my heart was bigger than my ego. I was mortally terrified that if I didn't take this leap of faith, I was truly committed to a hell of my own making.

So, I filled out two years' worth of bureaucracy and got my self- fingerprinted. I was claiming responsibility for my criminality. I would be absolved of all my past, by owning up to my future; my daughter.

HALEY

I take the halo from your head

I pour a prayer in a riverbed

I get my courage from a jar

Fireflies for you in Mars

Chorus

Stardust spinning from Saturn

Pluto, raining, windburn

Comets fly and deranged

Bursting into flames

Neon paves your path

A satin cloak in red and black

Cobwebs weave my guilt

A tapestry made in silk

Hovering high, side by side

Pulling back the tide

Pulling fear back to its root

A cradle rocks, its mute.

Chorus

I cast out my doubt, my sins

My black fishnets to pull you in

The fortress of my old wounds

Drifting, dragon balloons.

4.

DARKNESS MAKES ME STRONG

My mother was a brilliant, bi-polar woman. She went eight decades without a proper diagnosis. I just thought she was full of energy and too intelligent for her own good. In her lifetime, she had found her trades in nursing, psychology, financial management, selling retail, fund-raising, judging horticulture, ministry, and too many other categories too mention.

My father left her after she was sixty. She always ran on the maniac side, except for the year after my father divorced her. Only then, did her depression level her playing field.

She came from that 40's era, where she was first and her kids were reflections of her generation's achievements. She'd often mimicked her mother, "children are to be seen and not heard." I recently watched Mad Men and was so disturbed by the series, as it was verbatim my parent's relationship. Narcissism, country clubs, and high society were the backdrop of my childhood. It was the fuel that fed my mother's self-esteem.

She was crushed when they kicked her out of the club because of her divorce. Her gardening club left her a senior spot but the cocktail party invitations dwindled, as did her friends. She started playing bridge and took up a new career.

She detested her "old gang", criticized our generation, for our excessive riches. "All your friends are shooting up Botox, and getting their faces rearranged leaving them with no familial traits. It's disgusting!"

Then came "Ave". Avery, unknown to all of us, surfaced in her 79th year, after his wife of forty years passed. Mom had written her mandatory conciliatory, sympathy card; something that was automatic and not attached to emotion. She operated off a "grace guideline" that was etched into her brain by her mother. Her manners were impeccable, in juxtaposition to her tone and assumptions of those closest to her.

This widower was eager to get a replacement so he immediately phoned, courting her carefully into a swift marriage agreement. His own wife was buried in August and Mom was in NYC by December, to break the news to me, on the day of my father's eighty-third birthday. I wasn't sure if she accepted out of revenge at my father, or had completely lost her mind. Every sentence started with "Ave". Prior to "Ave" all her banter surrounded who had just keeled over on the golf course or what "dear friend" had 'bought it' at the banquet table over a platter of the escalloped potatoes.

Whatever the reason, her behavior had an ominous effect on my sisters and I, and there was massive discussion of intervention. Like all great maniacs, she shunned us at every attempt, placing "Ave" on an altar.

By January, he had moved in, accompanied by matching chaise lounge chairs. There was also a new love of architecture, as that was "Ave's" former vocation, so we were receiving bi-weekly architecture magazines, pointing out the tremendous line of some chapel or the ubiquitous shape of the domed assembly hall of some boarding school.

She had decided to dump her assets, leaving us to manage her estate, while she passed her final glorious years in North Carolina; a place she had never seen. Most alarming was that she was trying to book the National Cathedral for the big wedding.

It came as an utter thud when "Ave" was admitted to a local hospital with a headache, which turned into a hematoma, which turned into surgery, and then three weeks later, delivered death. My mother had posted all of her hospital visitor stickers on a bulletin board to prove she was loyal and true, awaiting his recovery so they could have their postponed engagement party.

After he died, she descended into darkness. I wrote this for her because there was no other way for me to reach her; words were out of the question.

HE FLIES BY

In a twist of fate, he arrived in a storm
Another twist he was gone without warning
The last leaf had turned to fall
She embraced him, like Christ at a ball.

She takes a check and to clear the claim
The 21stdebt left in his name
He pedaled love, she ushered him out
Two angels in a twist of clouds

Chorus
He flies by in the dusk of the evening
He's close by even when she's sleeping

Seagulls soaring the bay
Even lilies won't brighten her day
Her grief is grace turned inside out
He healed her heart and banished her doubt
Chorus

He flies by in the dusk of the evening
He's close by, even when she's sleeping
He's the sign of all her healing
He's her cross from all her kneeling

A billion kisses now planets away
He flies by even while she prays
A billion kisses and planets away
He flies by even while she prays.

Chorus

I am a huge admirer of men. I come from a family of all girls. I have aunts on both my parents' side. I went to an all-girl school from kindergarten through senior year. My childhood was saturated with women.

Naturally, the opposite sex was foreign to me. They were forbidden in our bedrooms. With the exception of my father of course, I did not know men. My father loved women. He had a million girlfriends.

I was shy and humbled by men. Their physique and personalities seemed monumental to me. If I liked a guy, he would never know because I wasn't the type to divulge my feelings. He might reject me, or worse, he might not even notice me.

I spent a great deal of time studying men. I gazed at lifeguards, with their gorgeous muscles and tans. I was fascinated by their bodies at wrestling matches, and equally amazed at their ability to lose weight for such occasions. When I was a wrangler in Wyoming, I loved to watch their backs move side to side as I followed them on long trail rides. Men playing guitars were tangible Gods.

I knew they were bigger, bolder, and brighter, and I wanted to be with them, hold them and have them crush me. I loved the power I had over them right before sex. They occupied my mind for endless hours in high school. Dreamy, pubescent boys replaced boring biology classes. I didn't need a chart to show me their anatomy. I wanted to touch them, study them, and squeeze them.

I have a friend who was a real glamour puss. She was the aphrodisiac to all men. Whenever she walked in a room, the men fell in suit, like dogs in heat. She put something out there, some kind of scent to let them know, she was game. I didn't know how to do that. I was not so alluring. I never walked up to a guy who I lusted after and said, "let's go." But I wanted to.

MEN

I like men who like Italian cars, men who smoke coheba cigars.

I like Petty, Eddie V. Surly men who admire me
I like men who hop out of planes, who jump the trains, ride in rain
I like guys who like to take their time, half feline, who are all mine.

I like men. I like men. I like men who come again
I like men. I like men. I like men

I like men who are guised with grace, shy and sweet, on the make.
I like guys who are soft inside, tough and mean, with half-massed
eyes.
I like guys who ride Harley bikes, who get in fights, for me at night.
I like men who drive diamond tractors, radio blasters, telecasters.

Chorus

Leaning towers of steel and slate
Crying out, hey baby, hey
Cooing pigeons at parks and lakes
Sitting on benches, waiting to mate

Chorus

Oh yeah, they drive me wild.
I just want to get a piece of their smile
Yeah, they drive me wild

come on baby stay for a while

I have listened to my husband's beautiful chords for years. He plays lush melodies while perusing the internet. His hands are always moving, even in his sleep. In the morning, when I drink my coffee, he studies some guitar, or obscure part he is eyeing on eBay. He is unaware of how many gorgeous melodies he is throwing away. I'm not. Two years into our relationship when I started writing songs prolifically, I started recording riffs he was not aware of playing.

He took little notice of this, as he was always consumed with melody, so there was no worry of his music drying up. His muse had hired him full time, and his favorite line was, "I haven't slept since the sixties."

Being the desperate type, constantly worried of where my next paycheck was coming from, I took ever melody seriously. I thought it would be my ticket to payday. Twenty years later, the most I ever made was five thousand dollars on a TV show.

This is not true for GE. He has always had opportunities banging on his door. He worked tirelessly for them as he started playing guitar at four. I worked tirelessly at hanging around those who worked tirelessly.

GE's dismissal of his original melodies fueled my desire to archive what he discarded. He was a musician for hire, not to be confused with crazy ideas about artistic endeavor. Here in lies my problem. I wrote for myself. He was there to entertain the masses.

I don't know if Frieda Kahlo and Diego Rivera ever collaborated, but this is one of GE and mine. We came from such different musical callings, he, steeped in historic blues and traditional songs; I was ultra-modern influenced by singer-songwriters from the seventies, eighties and nineties. He wrote this melody, except the bridge. I was always the bridge genius. I imagined what he might write.

DARKNESS MAKES ME STRONG

Hey, what's that you say
I can't obey, the way you may
Hey, turn off the lights
Try as I might, I lost my sight
Look, you're adrift
Feel the rift, there was a shift

Chorus
I'm a moon spinning on
darkness makes me strong
I'm a moon spinning on
darkness makes me strong

Hey, here's what I say

Those cards you played, relics fade

Hey, cut out those lights

This ain't no fight, it's safe at night

Look, I'm adrift

Water's swift, Sunkist

Adrift, water's swift, played, relics fade

Adrift, Sunkist, played, relics fade

Chorus

5.

MS THIRD PLACE

My parents divorced when I was a young adult; there were no twelve steps for that. There is no recovery from a fractured family, only a big hole to replace a sense of belonging. It's death without a funeral. There is no pill to remove the pain. I have watched my sisters grapple with the undoing of cohesion. We were their collateral damage and left for debris. We stayed in bad situations to protect our own children because we all knew what devastation would be inflicted on their souls if we changed course.

My parents came from a generation where they felt entitled to be free. They rebelled against their puritanical parents. They severed their histories and their legacies because they were encouraged to live it up. They were the ultimate consumers because they had survived the Great Depression. They were also supposed to follow "Donna Reed" down some hideous path of perfection that the advertising agencies conjured up, and of course, they fell short.

I am the result of their catastrophe. I am their very imperfect, broken, soul. I am an alien when it comes to trust. I was too shattered for repair but that did not stop me from loving my own family. It did not stop me from giving up the love I feel for my husband, my daughter, and my art. I do not resonate with defectors. I am a refugee trying to build a new life without the foundation of my original family. While there is no time for the past, it has shaped my future. This song was a calling for my parents.

WILD OLD FOOL

Lying by the fireside, staring thru the lace
I spotted a searchlight, and thought of your face
It conjured up the memories of my life's base
I felt my soul screaming at our human race

I still love you I still love you
I still love you, you wild old fools

Gazing at a sunset sparkling on the lake
A loon cried out for my broken spirit's sake

A warm caressing wind dried my little tears
Helped me wash away, the loss of missing years

Chorus

You think that I've forgotten the stage that you're at
I see your fear so clearly, I'm used to all that
You know I'd never turn my back I'd always let you in
I'm the mirror of your hope I'm fighting to win

I love you

My grandfather on my father's side was a steeplechase
rider with a penchant for Glen Livet. As a result, I have always
had an attraction to thoroughbreds and alcoholics. I had a Jungian
therapist who said I reminded him of a thoroughbred; wound tight,
but a white knuckling champion.

As a teenager I used to spend a lot of time in the fields with
horses, bailing hay, or swimming in rivers. Maryland countryside
was filled with marigolds and queen's breath in the springtime and
it was a perfect place for equestrians to pass time.

I spent my summers in Wyoming wrangling horses on a
ranch outside of Cody. I would take pack trips into the valleys and
prairies, by horseback. Once I'd reach the destination for the
evening, I would take of the bridal and saddle and let the horse

roam while I lay on its back, gazing at the fluffy clouds or clear blue skies.

The swaying of the horse's body, or the swishing of its tail, lulled me into a meditation. I felt so safe and nurtured by my horse. I feel the safest in nature and in the wilderness. Riding is the ultimate escape.

THOROUGHBRED

Crashing into corners, crashing in my bed
Black-eyed Arabian mourners, chanting in my head
My yard is full of foxes; my horse is in the barn
I got a call from Chachi, they're tearing down my farm

Chorus
I've got a thoroughbred, built to run the course
Can't rein in a volcanic force
Wild and untamed, committing every sin
a .44 bullet, skimming on the wind

Riding under bridges, riding way, way low
Got to cross the ridge, go, Sassafras girl, go
Fleeting fields, of golden hay, bloodhounds on my trail
Thumping, thumping hooves of black and gray, a whipping might entail

Chorus

He's always by my side
I can always ride
He becomes my limbs
We reel in the wind

Chorus

I have had the great fortune of meeting some of the most influential actors, musicians, writers, and dancers of the 21st century. I think I manifested that fortune by choosing a life in the arts and moving to New York City.

I was initially so dazzled by the brilliance of the celebrated artists and so intoxicated by the heights of emotion that I would feel when experiencing their talent, I often forgot that they were at an earlier time, the same as me; someone in search of being heard and someone in need of beauty.

Art is just another way of putting reality together. Economics could have been my true purpose but I didn't see how numbers would equate to melody. I didn't understand how statistics and buying trends would add up to a full heart. I was an avid hunter of the masterpiece.

I wake up every day with the hugest fear that I can't complete my masterpiece. I have not reached my full potential. I am holding out incapable of finding the right color or texture to complete my tapestry. I am terrified that I can't finish what my muses have asked of me. I am too broken and tired and I can't seem to assimilate their ideas in a practical way. My biggest fear is that I let God down. I was so busy trying to do the things that I was asked, like take care of my mother, listen to my sisters, serve my husband, be a good friend, what about my manners? there isn't enough time to travel, my daughter needs me, more than I need myself, and so on.

At the end of the day, I realize I need courage: courage to break the lifelong cycle of serving as second best; courage to break out of being condemned. So, this is my surrender. I am breaking the gorgeous Echo. I am breaking my loyalties to the Narcissist, my father. I will abandon my sisters to get this right. And I will stand alone on top of Mount Olympus.

MS THIRD PLACE

I'm pretty enough, girl next door
I'm skilled and tough, daily allure
They throw roses, but not at my feet
I stand, the triangle, and I concede

Held the course, towed the line

Performed it in Olympian time

Topped the charts, rode the crest

I surrender and I confess

Prizewinner, I thought

Proud of my face

As hard as I fought

I'm crowned Ms. Third Place

My spirit is worthy

My presence, unnerving

My grace, surprising

The tide keeps on rising

Chorus

Surrounded by genius and gods

Archangels draped in love

All around me, they feast in my yard

Tempt me and rip me apart.

6.

THE CALLING

We had just gone to dinner in Chinatown with a new group of friends. Expanding our circle of acquaintances, seem to be the gift of adopting our daughter. Our closest friends were all artists, so making idle banter with financiers felt challenging.

We arrived home later and I felt very anxious. I wasn't sure if it was the food, the company, or my then, seven-year-old having her first sleepover but I couldn't find sleep.

I was tossing and turning, awakening every five minutes. At around three, the full moon appeared like a searchlight, shining directly on GE's face. Having a skylight in New York City with a clear view of the moon was mesmerizing, but this moon was troubling; something was off.

The next morning, I decided to give GE some space, and took the little girls to the park. It was covered in snow and while they were busy making snowmen, I felt so much discomfort. I decided to take the girls to *MOMA* as art always soothed me and brought me a sense of calm.

We took in Monet and made our last stop at Cy Twombly on the third floor. I was explaining to my daughter that Cy was amazing but I thought Pollack was just hurling insanity on canvas. It was then I got the text. It read, "did I hear?"

It was with great sadness that I learned our longtime friend, GE's best bandmate, and our best man from our wedding had suddenly died of a heart attack. He had a congenital heart disease and always said he would just "up and go", but no one took it seriously. T-Bone had finished a day of tracking, checked on his elderly father, and at eleven, went home, sat in a chair, and pulled by the gravity of time, departed.

There is no doubt that I felt his passing and there was no doubt that he had shown the light, by way of the moon, on my husband's face.

I later learned at his memorial, Cy Twombly was his favorite artist. There stood his lumber jacket, hat, and Gibson hummingbird. All the great musicians of New York were there. I was overwhelmed by the talent that was in the room and how T-Bone was integral to the making of music of so many of the attendees.

HEARTACHE ON THE HUDSON

The moon has rose up and gone

The horns blare in early dawn

I hope today will be the change

I won't feel so deranged

Chorus

Another heartache on the Hudson

Another day to break this pain

The ghosts walk blindly

And our love blows up in flames

My thoughts rule my fears

I've shed all my tears

A shadow lurks behind

Is anyone ever kind?

Chorus

Wind carry me back to sea

Back to where I want to be

Take me back, back below

Back to where I want to go

Chorus

I do not know how long I thought my beloved father would live, but I found great comfort while visiting with him, in his 93rd year. I had come down to pick up our daughter from Foxcroft, a boarding school that resembled my childhood.

My father was quite fond of Foxcroft as his ancestors had hailed from Winchester, Virginia and later migrated to Baltimore after the Civil War. He knew the headmistress who had started the school and was proud his grandchild was learning our history.

My family was steeped in war and steeplechases. I have one of the ancestors' *wrist-breaker* swords hanging in front of my fireplace and an original letter of George Washington's.

My daughter, a tried and transplanted Manhattanite, was not so keen on Virginia. She experienced her first bout of racism, being adopted, of Asian descent. It was very complicated for her to explain to provincial Virginians, that no, she was not a) an Asian boarder from Beijing, but an American who was adopted and lived where they perceived "everybody was a "Kardashian". It was equally disturbing for me to really understand the depth of hate, teenage girls could unleash on those who were not cookie-cutter, white girls. I was brought up with privilege, but never tolerated racism or used it against someone. But, because I am a white woman who came from money, as hard as I might like to sympathize, I will never know how cruel it feels to be the recipient of racism.

We spent countless hours talking our daughter out of her despondency or rage, explaining that small-minded kids would always pick on those who seemed vulnerable, but their actions were on them, not her.

At any rate, after two grueling years, our daughter was returning home. Back to the bubble of New York, where tolerance was still practiced. I sent my daughter home with GE with a car packed with all her horse equipment.

Many of my songs have horse metaphors and they appear throughout my ten collections. My daughter was born in the *YEAR of the HORSE* in Changsha, China. I get very emotional when I see the horse's race or just feeding in a pasture. I am often found staring at the green pastures seeing mirages of ancient races.

Anyway, on this last visit to Virginia, I stayed behind to escort my father to one of our family's oldest, matriarch's memorial service. My father was in the middle stage of dementia, great long-term memory, not so good on recalling his last sentence, let alone me. Sometimes he would start speaking in gibberish. I assured him I understood.

The memorial was held at my father's country club. My daughter and husband had eaten at Elkridge countless times because my father liked the comfort of the food, even if it made him sick. The same bartender who served me Shirley temples as a kid, now ancient, was still serving drinks.

My father and I sat in the back, where I spotted old familiar faces. I wondered how I had gotten so far away from my roots. So many of my old acquaintances had stayed and habitually repeated their parents' lives. There was a prestigious picture of my Uncle on the wall and many more of horses riding through their hunts.

I stared through the windows at the old, oak trees, taking in the golf course, remembering dancing class, and parties my parents had thrown for their fortieth, fiftieth, sixtieth, and then, memorials for my mother, my friend's father, my sister.

I remembered many Saturday mornings when I would accompany my father to his office down on "the Block" which was the coined-phrase for where they hookers ran "their racket". My father never had a racist bone in his body and would often convene with some of the more colorful characters, even playing hoops with some of the pimps, if he could.

The scent I always associate with my father, is that of a stale industrial smell, which emanated from his business suit. His office was a mess with dust and paper flying everywhere and I would perch myself on his secretary, "Daisy's" seat, and pretend to take his orders.

I couldn't imagine what kind of work he was doing but I cherished my stolen hours with him. Sometimes, my sister Emilie would join and we would rifle through his graphic designers' art tools, making our own ads. Afterword, Dad would take us to "Ginos" for a .19 burger and then a visit to the Zoo.

Druid Hill Park would become a fixed memory for me as I was dropped off there every Saturday for four years where my father and another kind gentleman coached me into becoming a child-star-tennis player. I recanted all these memories while sitting quietly next to my father.

Back to that present moment, I took note of who was there that day of the memorial with my father and I, and how this matriarch had brought us together to celebrate her life; a life that was filled with kindness and generosity.

I listened to her sons talk about how strong a bond their family had, supporting four generations and I heard about how when the matriarch was in her eighties, she attended her great-grandson's lacrosse games routinely, even if they were eight hours away. My father sat quietly next to me while the sons' spoke of spending special times in *our lake* house in New Hampshire. A house my family had once spent many summers in too. Their family had so many meaningful moments in what had been *our family* summer home. *Our* family had memories of divorce and loss. Their family had laughter. We had tears and silence. Their family had children begetting more children. *Our* family lost all connection to each other.

I sat there with my father, the one person I was so afraid of losing, as he was the last tie to my hometown. I don't know why I was so afraid as I had long ago, buried the sadness of my broken family and embarked on my own, finding my anchor, in a rootless world. I wondered how my daughter felt, anchored in her rootless world. I wondered how I felt more loved by strangers than my own kin. I wondered, how will I know when I am safe? When can I stop running from the pain of a broken heart? When I will be at peace with the broken memories that run through my veins?

My father and I stumbled around the club and found ourselves seated across from each other, identical piercing blue eyes, gazing. I never knew if it was going to be the last time with my father and while I had so much to say, like, "How did we go from being your adored daughters to uninvited guests overnight?" or "I'm just like you because currently I want to run off with another man!" or "every night I wonder why I was ever born?" or "Dad, I am sorry I was an artist!." Instead we just stared at each other and complained about how cold the room was. Finally, I said, "well, Marion had a good life. Dad remarked, "don't order the lamb. It gave me the runs."

THE CALLING

On the moors, down by the graveyard
Where the rivers move like snakes
My tears are all past legends
My treasure laid to waste

In the fields, between the queen's breath
In the blades of bales of hay
All my kisses for a young lad
my stolen lost love lays

Chorus
Take the wind and mix my yearning
Take the dust laced with desire
Let the rain bring down the thunder
And the starlight sparks my fire

In the silence of the grey mist
In the dampness of the dawn
I forgave those that abandoned
Souls, sold, gone.

In a cabin where the embers

Paint our shadows on the wall

Where a spirit must surrender

To the rise and to the fall

Chorus

The calling, the calling, the calling, the calling, the calling

On the moors where the rivers move like snakes

My tears and my treasures lay to waste

7.

7 STEPS

My father told me he had re-occurring dreams of me. Something like I was always riding my bike too fast downhill and to his horror I always crashed. He ran down to see, what he thought would be the remains of me, only to find me, standing up, slightly soiled, laughing. What he didn't realize was I was just like him. Reckless, and redeemed. He always taught me to get back on the saddle, no matter how far down I had gone.

Why was I so reckless? I was not afraid of danger, and neither was he. A brave Baltimorean, my father stood at the helm of the City Planning Commission of Baltimore, while the town exploded in riots. My father taught me to get in the trenches with the down-trodden, less fortunate, to help lift them up for new opportunities. I have never been afraid of danger, just acquired fast thinking strategies when the light suddenly turned black.

In my mid-fifties, I decided to embark on a trip to India, with my best-friend Lavinia. She too, was not afraid of danger. We both had moved to Paris together when we were twenty and learned how to navigate foreign territory while finding our callings; mine dance, Lavinia's, a Frenchmen.

We had split up after landing in Delhi. She went to Rajasthan, while I headed to Bangalore. She had a guide, I had myself. She had her children and I had my singing and writing tools.

After thirty hours of travelling, the plane circled Bangalore with a spectacular lightning storm. I thought if the plane goes down, what a beautiful display of India's skies. How lucky am I to see this as my last sight?

And that is the way I look at every dangerous situation. Not that it is dangerous, but what about it is beautiful while it is unleashing its terror on me.

My father always barked at me, "There's nothing to fear, but fear itself." A homily he picked up from a former President to encourage me to challenge myself beyond my comfort zone.

When I landed, I was picked up by a beautiful Hindu man who had black smoky, sexy eyes. I was truly intrigued by him and wondered what it would be like to sleep with him; especially since we had no words to communicate with. He was dressed in a sari and smelled of burnt fire.

I took a yoga retreat and received Ayurveda treatments. This was of course designed to bring me balance and peace. I had embarked on this in hopes of getting past the grief of losing my sister, Blair.

I spent time in this hollowed out sanctuary that was in the middle of a bustling city. The natives worshipped thousands of different deities, twenty- four hours a day. I thought I might be blessed just by osmosis and it didn't matter where I laid my sins. Surely one of the revered would grant me joy. And this was how it worked.

I spent days writing, doing yoga, sightseeing, drifting through spice markets in Bombay, riding boats in the Arabian Sea, and hanging out with Saudi Arabians in posh Goa. God was good. Until I got to the airport to go home.

I had left my cell phone in a van on the way, and somehow managed to track the driver down, and decided since I was so late I better wave down a rickshaw.

He took one look at me and a sinister smile beckoned me in. I had no choice. There was a gathering group of other men who were hip to the fact that I was lost and descending on me.

I jumped in the rickshaw and he took me immediately into the slums. I fired off a text to my husband that I was in trouble and began to think what to do. Calmly, I suggested he just drop me off, but he was having none of that. So, I looked at my hands. I had a fake emerald ring that looked real. I said, "well, what about this?" I could give you this for a ride to the right terminal.

He said, "the ring and $1000."

I said, "I only have $700."

"Deal."

I had two thousand but I realized that I was going to need something to get home if something else happened. And it did.

He dropped me off at the bottom of the highway ramp which led to the airport, so I had to haul my suitcase up, running, to try to make the flight

I had. I was very late. When I got to the ticket counter, breathless, the lady told me I didn't have a ticket.

"Absurd," I said.

"No seat in your name."

She hauled me off to the superiors. They said, 'for a fee' they might be able to get me a ticket on another plane going to another country.

I stood my ground. "Nope," I said. "I want a first-class ticket on the plane I was booked on."

They argued for another thirty minutes, then charged me two thousand extra dollars and booked me in the last row of the plane in the scummiest seat for a sixteen- hour ride back to JFK.

I was so shaken I was awake the entire trip.

When I came too, after breaking out in hives, the following day, I called American Express to press charges. Air India was fined and apparently the entire crew in Bombay was fired too.

The beauty of being kidnapped; I saw the slums first hand and was so glad I was an American with an American Express Card.

WIND

I am wind that shifts with time

I don't land I can be blind

I am gentle like a touch

I'm a traitor who will rough you up

I am wind that has no home

I have no anchor, no solid bones
I'll crush the waves etch the clouds
I'll slam Irene in the mouth

Chorus
It's like they say, I'm passing by
An ominous voice in the sky
I have no ties to this life
I'm a monk at midnight

I know in truth I can't be held
Like the fading sound of church bell
I am a curious witness
Delivering furious kisses

Chorus
Its' like they say I'm tough to bear
A cruel stranger in the air
I have no time no constant friend
I cause the danger and the end

I'm the wind kicked up by a car
I'm the tiller of a shooting star
I am the calm in the breeze
I man the seasons the ebb and bleed

Fourth of July has always been a bittersweet holiday for me. It brings early childhood memories of tradition. It was my parents' anniversary and my grandmother's birthday so we would always be expected to celebrate both, instead of Independence Day.

We would probably start the day off at Elkridge Club, swimming. If it fell on a Thursday, it would mean I would be in the weekly swim race and expected to win. I always won to please my father and have a stack of trophies to prove it. The way I won everything is, I never took a breath and this allowed me the advantage over my other counterparts, who paused to breathe.

I think I have run my career and life in the same manner. Never pausing to breathe, might someone surpass my ambition. Anyway, the fourth of July was marked with deviled eggs and dubonnet in my grandmother's garden, followed by fireworks at a nearby neighbors, (the Brooks) with fried chicken and Pepsi.

I hated the explosions. It scared me. I cringed at the bright lights and was terrified at each bolt of thunder. I think I closed my ears and eyes to get through the perfunctory yearly viewing. I cowered under my father's arm and imagined what people felt like in a warzone.

At night, when we finally were spent and went to bed, my mother would kiss all of us, reminding us, that on each anniversary we were made. My sisters and I had birthdays in April so it was her way of showing us that we were created out of the celebration of their anniversary.

I think that was probably the only time they made love as my father had other woman who he had spent more time with, between the sheets. I guess I thought the fourth of July was a day of rest for my father who might be noted as "a sex addict" now, but in those days was gloriously touted as a *philanderer*.

Woman flocked to my father. It didn't matter where we were, there was always a desperate, attractive housewife, drooling over Dad. My mother took little notice because affairs were tolerated and not to be mentioned in her generation. As her daughter, I learned to tolerate the unwanted intrusions as well.

I have always had a long leash for abhorrent behavior because of this. It didn't matter how unattractive the situation I was in, I managed to see the good in wherever I was, even though, the situation was clearly intolerable. Subsequently, I've spent Fourth of July's with memories I'd rather forget.

It took me a lifetime to see how my father had taught me to be a good con woman. He was an ace when it came to getting people to do things for him for free. He didn't believe in building pools in our backyard. When the neighbor next door had one, he just built a ladder over the fence and screamed with glee, "get your suits on girls!"
If there was a sign that said 'No Entrance', Dad would sashay right in and with a grin, "follow me!" If there was someone not so pleased by his behavior, he would slide them a dollar or give them a compliment which dismantled their annoyance. There was nothing that would block my father's path when he had a desire.

When I went to College, he knew I was not the best at following rules because naturally I took after him. He gave me a green VW and switched out the VW emblem on the bumper with a BMW emblem. This was amazing foresight.

I racked up four years' worth of parking tickets in Burlington, Vermont, when I'd leave my car anywhere but in a proper parking zone. As the traffic violations accumulated in my mailbox and eventually followed to my parents' residence for the numerous citations, my father called me and smirked; "those idiots don't know the first thing about shit! Now march into that station and show them that you don't have a BMW and point out that the car is registered as a Volkswagen!"
Meekly, I did what I was told and all was dismissed. I was my father's best student and I took this terrible habit of fleecing people with me into my adulthood. I was always looking for ways to cut corners, get it for free, nickel and dime people, and as one of my bosses later reported, "she could shake money out of a tree!'

My con artistry became an asset for my employers because they knew I had the ability to charm people to do things for me. Most people had better etiquette or were taught to do business by the books but I was taught to take whatever I could. I think this trait drifted down from my father's mother who was a fast-talking, conniving, beauty who grew up dirt poor in Richmond Virginia.

She broke into a Debutante Ball and lassoed my rich grandfather and elevated herself to Queendom. She taught my father the ins and outs of naughty behavior and did it with a sense of humor. Shenanigans were rewarded with laughter around my house. My grandmother was a real character. I resemble her in size and stature.

HIM

U walk coyly to Sinatra's beat

I'm still groovin' to 'dancing in the streets'

Trilling horns keep your step so light

Bob Weir kept me trippin' all night

Chorus

We're going down and it's hard to believe

We're from the same town playing minor keys

Nightmares and demons engulf my mind

dancin' it up on Goodman time

It's all positive, celebrate

Not my bleeding heartache

Chorus

Bassline thumping at your heart

I'm stuck, hurt, torn apart

High-hat mimics your cool demure

I'm behind an underscore

Bow ties, bold, capitals gains

Blue jeans, small, up in flames

Bloodlines circling at a fair

I'm running on empty with the snare

Chorus

Going down and it's hard

I rode my bike down the waterway today. I have been riding my bike or running down this path for over forty years. I love the way the water shimmers with sparkles or the way a black storm comes in from the Gulf.

Forty years ago, I was carefree and wild. I arrived my first time, after Christmas, freshman year to stay with my ex-boyfriend and his friend. My ex was not really that keen on seeing me so I made my way across the narrow bridge and discovered paradise; Palm Beach.

I met up with my good friend from college, Lavinia. Lavinia's mother had rented a house and Lavinia was my introduction to high living. Born and bred from a wealthy New York City family, she gave me the long list of must- haves. "Fracas, Janet Sartin, Calvin Klein jeans, Louis Vuitton, Pierre Joeut and Lanvin gowns."

She opened my eyes to a whole new world and she taught me how to seek men's desire. It was all about allure and letting them know, there was a possibility to be led to the bed, but not a guarantee.

Later, we spent a half a year in Paris together, where I fine-tuned my dancing skills and learned to strut my stuff. We both always returned to Palm Beach and coincidentally, my father was so swayed by my enthusiasm, he abandoned Fort Lauderdale and investigated. He loved it, just like I did.

He then divorced my mother, took up with a woman fifteen years younger and embarked on his second, better life. He bought a cute little cottage on the north end of Palm Beach across from the Kennedy compound. He was often mistaken for Ted Kennedy as he had similar looks.

Year, after year, he would convene for some part of some season to this illustrious, decadent playground, and watch Rolls Royces, Jaguars, and Bentleys parade down Royal Poinciana. This was all before West Palm Beach and the bourgeois arrived.

Worth Avenue was dripping with worldwide socialites and the only place to really eat was the Bath and Tennis Club or the Everglades. The Breakers was its own city not really a part of the charm of Palm Beach.

Palm Beach has always felt like home to me.

Palm Beach allows me to forget who I thought I was supposed to be. I can wander anonymously being my father's daughter. Whenever I arrive I drop my ambitions and settle down. I notice the shape of an old Banyan tree and allow myself to let go of my driven will. I feel my bones unwind and I feel young again. I don't care what I look like and I don't care what other people think of me. It's the antithesis of who I am in New York.

I wish I had learned to relax and not have to be so insecure without achieving some level of success. I have always been highly vigilant in diet, exercise, and spiritual acuity. This allowed me to keep one step ahead of others. I was always on high alert.

My fear of being unattractive to others was tantamount. I don't know why. I look around at so many people and they are perfectly happy with their appearance. They don't care about extra weight. They are not worried about financial insecurity. I am uber responsible. Who's going to judge me. God?

I am now at the age where my sex appeal is unimportant. I went to a yoga class today and noticed a very cute married man, older, greying, and courageous enough to just 'be'. I was attracted to that.

I wonder what kind of effect I have on others. Everyone has an effect, good or bad, and I wonder how the world experiences Taylor Barton. I am sure that there is a sense of opportunity with me. I offer anyone who comes into my orbit, a glimpse of a better future. I have always been that way.

I wonder if people can sense the underlying sadness I feel most all the time?

My daughter is annoyed as she sees me as divided. Only half there. I am totally there. I just am listening to the dreams in my head, at the same time I am listening to my daughter's need for my full attention.

If I am in a room and a song is playing, especially a song I like, I go into the song, and abandon the banter. I am a melody magnet. I am following the melody line until someone turns the music off.

Each time I come to Palm Beach, I feel a little closer to home or the home I once knew. My real home went up in smoke when my parents divorced and their new homes never felt comfortable. Their arrangement after the divorce worked great for them but left my siblings and I anchorless. Homeless. Yes, we had our homes, but our childhood memories were bombed.

Since my father has lived in Palm Beach for almost 30 years, and my best friend, I feel a huge level of comfort because it conjures up happy times for me. Or a place I find refuge. It is my sanctuary.

My best friend's brother lives here too and I have always had a crush on him. When I turned 55, we were at a party, and I was dancing wildly, as I always do, and he told me he had always wanted to get together.

I was stumped by this as I had no idea he liked me as well, but his wife would have me crushed, if I touched her man. It would be messy and my safe harbor would become a danger zone. But isn't that always the condition of love? You have to destroy mundanity to reach the heights of passion.

7 STEPS

Chorus
7 steps down,
I'm almost found
7 steps up,
I'm almost in love

I pictured of a meadow, covered in white
Walked thru the sage, and golden light
Stood by a stream, where the Indians bathed,
Cleansed my body, and prayed for a day
Chorus

Heard the whisper of the hailing wind

There's a man there, disguised as a sin

He's pining for you, says the astral charts

You'll know when u see him, by the beat of your heart

Been a dark horse, for most of my life

Relying on no one, throwing the dice

I'll stop my running to be adored

And lay in your arms forever more

8.

I'M THE ANGEL YOU TURNED AWAY

My mother left me the most beautiful bounty for an inheritance. Anyone in their right mind would have been overwhelmed with the magnitude of wealth I was bestowed. But I am not of the right mind; I am, of the left. I went from living in a small cottage, fully paid, to owning five houses with a bank account that swelled to seven figures.

It was very difficult for me to assume a different role. One that required me to figure out how to handle such abundance and a new challenge of responsibility; managing money. Simply, I hated it.

I longed for my life of deprivation. Everyone always assumed I was rich because GE was famous, but GE was not interested in cash. He was interested in cigars and guitars.

Furthermore, my complicated relationship with my mother made me feel guilty to own anything she had accrued. I liked to fly under the radar. Now, I was more visible. I sold five of my mother's properties and put it into one amazing chateau, hidden in the woods of Amagansett.

This period of time coincided with Trump's election and it became very apparent who was a democrat and who sided with *"America Being Great Again."* Both parties were despicable. The underlying hatred was seething from one house to the next. I sided with those who marched with the picket signs that said, "if you keep all the immigrants out, who is going to build the wall?"

It became painfully clear that a covert genocide was beginning. Trump was at the helm of ethnic cleansing and decimating freethinkers into silent witnesses.

While in Palm Beach, I was constantly told by leftists, "watch what you say." I thought of the beginning of the Holocaust when the first Jews were being interrogated or kidnapped. The others, thinking, wow, I hope this is contained to a marginal few. It is stunning that our generation who learned that these atrocities were hideously heinous, were voting and supporting a regime that was and is systematically trying to erase history.
And like all dictators, he is a sociopath.

My daughter and I visited Anne Frank's house in Amsterdam. It was a chilling experience to walk through the rooms, up the secret staircase, and into the small spaces that she and the six others occupied for two years.
I do not understand those voters that are trading our freedom for a man who, at best, will leave his office in Washington with the stock market in ruins. I refuse to be for or against. I am not going to give up my freedom in the names of guns, oil, and coal.
My mother left the world in time, and the greatest gift she gave me, was the means to flee.

I have spent many a morning at the Cross Sound Ferry listening to NPR after a gig somewhere in the Northeast. Always arriving at eight am to get the first ferry home on a Sunday, exhausted after singing somewhere, I tune into the weekend news.

I remember in the nineties a show that went on about how the new century was going to emulate fame, versus artistry. I couldn't understand why everyone thought fame was going to be the go-to and why artistry was going to take a second place. I was proud to cultivate an artistic platform that did not require celebrity. So, I had no idea that the internet was going to give way to the Kardashians, or the stars of Instagram. Even the gruesome terrorist Brenton Tarrant's rampage on the Mosque in New Zealand was streaming live.

There was the industrial revolution, the technology revolution that gave birth to the neo-Maoism, and white supremacists fueled by Fat Donny. Gone are the liberal ideas once expressed by my generation and the baby boomers.

I am living in a horror show of reversed history. Will they soon be fascists who will burn the books of liberalism?
As I sat at the ferry, looking at a boat that has run its course daily, unchanged by the political trends, but definitely a potential spot for terrorism, I wondered why our lives have gone so astray.

Who are these people that regurgitate hate? How has ignorance penetrated the American population? Where is the pride for freedom of speech and where are the politicians who can lead rather than destroy?

I have an emergency fund that would allow me to pick up and move to another country if I needed to, and I would if it meant I was unable to pursue the life I came on this planet to live.

Gunning down anyone in prayer is obscene. This surely is not God's will for anyone.

First, they came for the socialists, and I did not speak out—because I was not a socialist.

Then they came for the trade unionists, and I did not speak out—because I was not a trade unionist.

Then they came for the Jews, and I did not speak out—because I was not a Jew.

Then they came for me—and there was no one left to speak for me.

Martin Niemöller

No one wants trauma and it usually arrives without warning. I am talking about sudden death.

After three hellish years with my husband when he was working for a hellish artist, I was ready to walk. I had separated from GE but not filed a formal separation. I was getting back on my feet and had rented a tiny basement apartment for my daughter and I, and we were in a temporary spot waiting to move in.

It was Josie's first day of fourth grade; hot and hazy in the city, rainy, with the city's grim sticking to my bare legs. I went to Chinatown to buy cheap towels and was on my way home, when I got a message from my brother-in-law. Not liking this man, as I knew he was cheating on my oldest sister, I ignored his message.

Blair had helped me formulate a plan to get a divorce. She had coaxed me back to sanity when I was ready to kill my husband for cheating on me. She was trying herself to start a new life and she was my only ally when I was decimated.

GE was with Josie that day, trying to help heal the family, trying to implement normalcy, getting her back to school. We had just moved in all our luggage and my father called. I answered.

He said, "Tay, Blair is dead."

I screamed.

How could Blair be dead? I just talked to her last week. The facts my father conveyed were unclear. Something like, "a kidney stone sent her to the hospital, and she was recovering, fine in the morning, then dead in the street."

Sheer terror. It was beyond shocking.

Josie came home and saw my face. "What's wrong?"

"Aunt Blair is gone!" Not possible! Not so! I could not wrap my mind around these facts. I boarded a train to Maryland where more chaos and confusion escalated. Her husband had a forty-five- minute diatribe that he told every single person who walked into the house. Blair's daughter seemed to be in a flat state, unable to emote.

Her husband's matter of fact attitude, not wanting a service for her, not knowing where the hell her body was, seemingly happy, none of this made sense.

It was a cruel joke. It was a botched, cover up. Blair left a long-scrawled note that I found by her bed. In it, she wrote of how bad her relationship with her husband was, how violent he got. How he ignored her and fought with their daughter.

The last conversation she had with me, a week prior to her death, was about missing twenty-five thousand dollars of cash from her Farmer's Market. She thought her assistant had stolen it.

I found it in her husband's top drawer, the day I arrived.

Over the next three years, my brother-in-law inherited everything. He spent the money that was left to my niece. He alienated us and I was never allowed in her house again. He took it over and occupied it with his new girlfriend, a lawyer.

My sister was in agony at the end of her life. She was a mother to me and I will never understand how someone who was so generous and kind to all, would end up dead in the street outside her home.

"Pulmonary embolism," they said.

My brother-in-law sued the hospital too, and got a settlement for her life. My sister's life was worth a million times more, than the hell she was put through. I finally had the courage to listen to my brother- in-law's message.

"Tay, Blair is dead."

WHERE DID YOU GO

I sat on a bench, thinking of you

Imagining all the things we could do

A boat ride at dusk, carousel lights

Starry skies and the sweet good nights

Chorus

Where did you go, and the dreams I once knew?

I'll never know, you took them with you

A bleeding angel, a fleeting thorn
You left the world in a blinding storm
Sat on a bench screaming a prayer
Looking for you in the salty air
Chorus

There's no way to say how sorry I am
To not intervene in the merciless plan
Your love meant the most if only to brief
Rest my love, rest in peace

Chorus

One songwriter I have long admired is Rosanne Cash. She writes beautifully and eloquently without any extra words or music weighing down her message. I had the great fortune of studying with her and having her constant mentoring during my entire career.

I did not realize how hard it was to enter the world of music. Rosanne shared a rich history with her father and step-mother, Johnny Cash and June Carter. She had the amazing education of real musicians teaching her the craft and she knew how to pass that along.

To be heard and validated by a Grammy-winning songwriter was a drug I had never experienced. I always had confidence and faith in my other abilities which were first and foremost being a great jazz dancer and champion tennis player. Suddenly, I was looking up to someone I wanted to be. In the process, I abandoned myself.

I would run everything by her and she would patiently guide, advise, or steer me towards better words, better melodies, better clothing, better organizations to support, and in the most profound way, help me to be a better mother.

I moved into her basement right before I adopted my daughter. I was so afraid I would be a bad mother because I had such a bad relationship with my own mother.

I didn't realize I had transferred my need for an older sister when I no longer had my siblings around me. My sister, Blair, had mothered me and when she died, I still had not learned to mother myself.

I lived and listened to her world for ten years. I heard her children's footsteps pound across my ceiling. I heard the beautiful music she and her husband played.

I just wanted someone to love me and I thought if I would be a good enough songwriter, they would. But that is not what I do best. What I do well is far greater than anything else she could do for me. I go into the wilderness of life where most fear to tread. I didn't have a family in show business to follow and I had the courage to always follow my heart. My biggest regret is that it took me sixty years to find that out about myself. She covered one of my songs when we first met. She didn't have to, but she did.

I danced to her singing the song I wrote for a performance art piece in a show somewhere in Queens. How many people have the luxury of dancing to the beauty of their own words, sung by the wonderous Rosanne Cash?

I AM THE ANGEL YOU TURNED AWAY

I thought your love was meant for me

I thought your soul could set me free

I thought you wanted me to stay,

I am the angel you turned away

The road had reached an empty end

I was waiting to help you mend

I'll be gone by light of day

I am the angel you turned away

I am the angel you overlooked

I am the angel when you were hooked

I am the angel this union lacks

A bleeding angel, baby, you combat

Chorus

You will hear me calling in the wind

You'll break the law I forgive you sins

You will see my form within the mist

I am the angel now in Bliss

You sit stunned in a hopeless haze

I tried to help you through the maze

I'll light a candle to guide my way

I am the angel you turned away

I am the angel you turned away

9.

LAST TIME

I saw a show on Netflix that was deeply disturbing to me. It was *The Disappearance of Madeleine McCann.* Madeleine went missing from Praia Du Luz, Spain while her parents ate dinner approximately the distance of a football field away from the bedroom.

I had to ask myself why was I so haunted? Reason one; I thought I saw her while working in the San Francisco area. We were in Oakland at the Zoo and I had my daughter with my on a chairlift that oversaw the giraffe sanctuary. Right behind me, two gay guys were in line with a little girl, whom I immediately thought was Madeleine McCann. I knew it was her because of the abnormal iris in her eye.

I rode the lift shocked, pumped with adrenaline asking myself what to do? Once off, I confronted the gatekeepers at the Zoo and said we needed to contact the authorities.

No one wanted to get involved. I followed the couple and child around in a gift shop but finally gave up, leaving guilty and ashamed. Maybe I could have made a difference?

I did not know the facts of the case but it seemed at that time highly plausible that she could have been kidnapped for an illegal adoption ring. She was beautiful and bright and probably would garner a massive purchase from a desperate, wealthy family. How did I know this? Because I adopted a child from China and all the information I was given, was false.

The two gay men, quite possibly, did not know she was Madeleine McCann. However, they fit a perfect scenario of a couple who might seek a foreign outlet to secure a child.

Did it bother me because I don't know the true facts of my own child's adoption? Did I buy from a corrupt ring?

I never believed that she was abducted for a sex trafficking ring but rather an adoption ring. Perhaps, I can't fathom the sick pervert who would desire to sexually abuse a three-year-old. It makes more sense that she would be taken for the high auction price she would be given.

What is more disturbing, is the town knew that there were predators and sex trafficking rings operating in daylight and did nothing to protect their children to facilitate tourism trade. Rather, they focused on hiding the facts and their corrupt police system, and manipulated the evidence to point at the family.

Two weeks prior to Madeleine's abduction there was a predator who broke in and sexually abused a sleeping child. A week before several men were canvassing houses for children, under the guise of asking for donations for an orphanage that didn't exist. Weird men were lurking on the beach and everyone had reported it.

What makes me sad is that people came on a holiday expecting to be safe and protected on the grounds of the hotel and protected by the government. With a corrupt government for the sake of tourism, that was an impossibility.

FOR THOSE AMONG US

I always was an avid fan
Chance had it, I made a stand
No more shadows in the wings
I took the stage to change and sing

Chorus
I stand for silence I stand for youth
For those among us who hold their truth
I stand for those who have no choice
For those among us who have no voice

I saw the push that caused the fall
She died and he beat the law
Stolen lives and broken hearts
The hunter likes to rip apart

Chorus

The worlds gone crazy, erupted in fire
I hold my words and avoid the liars

Chorus

The power lies in the steady gaze

Hidden in a silent maze

It's not the loudest chant on the streets

It's given to those who never speak

I stand

I am sitting at my father's desk in my hometown while he is declining in hospice. He is diminished to bruises, bones and delirium. His piercing blue eyes gaze at me with determination to remain at the helm of his life.

Death has no boundaries. It takes and hijacks everything. I feed my feeble father pieces of chocolate I brought back from Switzerland and play Doris Day and Nat King Cole to ease his soul. I hold his hand and tell him stories of his champion days on the tennis court or describe the fun with used to have at the 'Baltimore Bullets' watching *Earl the Pearl*'.

I scan an article that says Baltimore's Harborplace is being invaded by hoodlums. These teenagers are not hoodlums but have posted a call- to-action to oppose the ever- increasing racism that is mounting again in Baltimore.

I am sad for my father because he dedicated his life to create 'The Harborplace'; a place that brought the community together and gave downtown Baltimore a space where all races could commune in harmony. My father was a good man. He was mischievous, yes, but he served in illustrious ways.

I stroke his face. It is so unfair that he is in this place where they are slowly killing him with morphine. He spent his entire life sober but he now is in so much pain, it is the only recourse.

I know all about morphine, as GE was a heroin addict for many of our married years. I despise the drug. And yet at the same time, I want the drug because I am not sure I can take another huge blow after losing my mother and sister. I have no choice. I am powerless to everything and everybody.

I drive around my old hometown, past my grandmother's house and my father's childhood home. I miss them all. It's a tsunami of grief. I have barricaded myself in another life to survive the loss of my original family. I will be forever a ghost in Baltimore once Dad is gone. No original family member lives here anymore. There is nothing worse than being a relic of a long line of Bartons.

THE WHEATFIELDS

In a dream that drifts just before dawn
In the valley of the kings
On a prairie east of a vacant farm
Stands a man I'm missing

I'm lying on a stolen horse
Waiting on Clementine
Exposed and naked with no recourse
Weak and alive

Chorus
Out beyond the mundane ideas
Right and wrong don't matter
I'll meet you in the sweet wheatfields
Kiss all that's shattered

Worn and used what's ahead
I fear I've been taken or cursed
A new day buries what was dead
I'm forgiven and alert

Chorus

Can I let go, is he in the know?
Can I survive, was I his valentine?

Hanging, waiting for him to appear
Tacked up my colt, to head home
I'm treading slowly, rescue is near
In the meadow of skull and bones

Dad is gone. I just made it to his bedside. He lays as if he has posed one last question. I don't know how to answer his question or how to live without him. In the end of his life, he was constantly harping about 'morals and standards'. I wasn't quite sure what that was referring to. He was gallant and classy. I was bohemian and adventurous. He rarely ventured out of a country club. I traversed the globe. He wore bow ties and complained of having "party toe" from too many black-tie events. I complained of being overworked as a producer of such events.

I am flooded by a myriad of family memories as I drive through all the familiar streets tending to his death. I drive by my childhood house and down the alley where my sisters and I waited every day for a thunderstorm. Once the storm started we would slather Prell in our hair, then run and splash in the puddles while letting the torrential rain rinse out the shampoo.

I imagine us all at the dining room table. My father and Blair seated at opposite ends, my mother across the table; Mandy seated to my right and Emilie across the way; for several years, a family unit.

I drive through the country where all the horses graze waiting for the next season of foxhunts and steeplechases. I know every curve of each road and remember every house as if I were still fifteen.

I head out to the graveyard where my father will be buried. It is the same place my grandparents are buried and there are six remaining plots that were supposed to be for the six of us.

I was also married in this church in the eighties to my first husband. Every day, for a week after that, I dreamed I was wearing a black wedding dress. I did not know then that I would be coming to this same chapel to memorialize my father. The dream was a psychic omen that I now understand was foreshadowing of my father's funeral.

I am overwhelmed by the memories and am equally terrified that the family fragments are not enough to sustain me.

Unexpectedly, my ex-brother-in-law had invited my sister and I to stay in my deceased sister's house as he was now, living with his girlfriend. My niece, who has barely spoken two words in the nine years since Blair died, was away.

I enter the house and it is as if Blair never left. Her paintings and her furniture remain. Her daughter has the same penchant for hoarding and has her clothing and stuff littered all over the first floor. Her daughter is not speaking with her father anymore. I am scared because I really don't know what exactly happened in the last few days of my sister's life and I don't want to find out now. I am too crushed by my father's death and can't shoulder much more trauma. Sleeping in Blair's guest room I am oddly comforted that I can let go of the enormous guilt that has been ravaging my mind and body since she died. I am at peace and I sleep hard. I dream that I am swimming in my sister's pool and imagine her speaking to me while I do my laps. She whispers how she died, but I can't hear her.

The next morning my sisters fly in for Dad's funeral. They are at each other with one's latest text saying "fuck off" to the other. This is the new language of my siblings. None of us are strong enough to battle this. We are obliterated from all the anguish and misery.

On the last morning that my father was alive I was riding my bike and had a final conversation with Dad in my head. "Dad", I said. "You have laid many obstacles for me. You caused me a lot of pain. Your weakness for women will leave us tied to your addiction forever, but you have made me strong and despite the horror of it all, I love you more, than not." I believe this was our last metaphysical contact. He departed while listening to Ella Fitzgerald singing, "Unforgettable You."

While my father had a charmed life and saw us as albatrosses, he set about making things right for me. He knew I would find the strength to take on any opponent. He knew I would rise to any occasion

and stand like all my southern ancestors; soldiers who took charge in

'the Battle of the Great Bridge'. Why did he know this? Because I am my

father's daughter and I, just like him, am now in charge.

LAST TIME

Last time I saw you, you said good bye

I knew it was over by the look in your eye

I tried so hard to forget

The kaleidoscope of my regrets

My world is big, does that make you small?

I can't be held down, I'm an outlaw

My mind is trapped by your fear

Your memory has no place in here

Chorus

A lucid dream takes me to the edge

the sunlight gleams on a river bed

Happy, alive, on the hunting grounds

On the Western Run of my home town

Summer or love, wind, rain

Nothing but the sound of a midnight train

I know I'll never feel you again

Was it just a mirage, my long-lost friend?

Chorus

I'm broken with not much to do

And I'll never get over losing you

The sorrow sits like a guest who won't leave

And I'm waiting patiently to be freed

Last time I saw you, you lay alone

Nothing but ashes and a heart of stone

THE END

Aftermath

I finished this novel in the summer of 2019. I recorded the audiobook during the pandemic of 2020 and was astonished that during this time, my friend coincidentally sent me a picture of Dexter King (Martin Luther King's son) right before the George Floyd murder. My father would have been so gratified by the worldwide dedication to the "BLACKLIVESMATTER" movement. He inspired me to stand for the rights of all and worked his whole life to integrate Baltimore's community. I inherited his beliefs and deeply want to end racism.

Acknowledgements
First and foremost
Cynthia Daniels
Monk Music Studios

I want to thank the amazing, talented musicians who have joined me over thirty years of recording and playing.

Sarah Jarosz, Andy York, Paul Ossola, Shawn Pelton, Alex Alexander, Steve Holly, Krishna Bhatt, Rob Fahey, Erin Hill, Mike Nolan, T-Bone Wolk, Christine Ohlman, Jon Carin, Jeff Kazee, Bob Funk, Paul Griffin, Jerry Vivino, Jenni Muldaur, Dana McCoy, Erik Della Penna, Josh Dion, Tony Shanahan and MOST IMPORTANTLY, G.E. Smith
My heart is your heart.

Other Books

by Taylor Barton

Hotheaded Saints   IUNIVERSE

Pedro 'n' Pip   IBOOKS